Disney MUSIC Activity Book

An Introduction to Music

Compiled and Edited by
Sharon Stosur

ISBN 978-1-4584-0258-5

WONDERLAND MUSIC COMPANY, INC.
WALT DISNEY MUSIC COMPANY

DISTRIBUTED BY

HAL•LEONARD®
CORPORATION

7777 W. BLUEMOUND RD. P.O. BOX 13819 MILWAUKEE, WI 53213

In Australia Contact:
Hal Leonard Australia Pty. Ltd.
4 Lentara Court
Cheltenham, Victoria, 3192 Australia
Email: ausadmin@halleonard.com.au

Visit Hal Leonard Online at
www.halleonard.com

Hi! My name is Mickey Mouse, and this is my *Disney Music Activity Book*. We're going to have lots of fun together. We'll learn about music and play and sing some of my favorite Disney songs. If you've seen our movies or visited any of the Disney theme parks, many of these songs will be familiar to you. In addition to the songs there are plenty of games, puzzles, and other activities for you to enjoy.

If this is the first time you've ever learned about music, that's okay! We'll start at the beginning. Minnie, Donald, and my other Disney friends will be here to help. You can also ask a grownup to join you in the fun.

Speaking of fun, let's get started!

Contents

Notes

When people sing or play a musical instrument, the sound they make can be written down with musical symbols called *notes*. The notes can be put together, one by one, to make a big piece of music, like a song.

Imagine that each note is a bead. The same way you can put beads together to make a beautiful necklace, you can put notes together to make music.

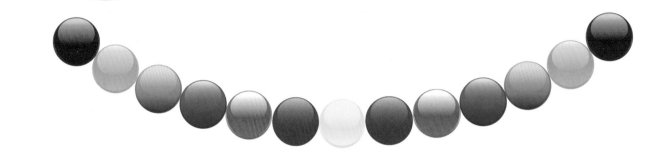

Some notes sound *high*; some notes sound *low*.

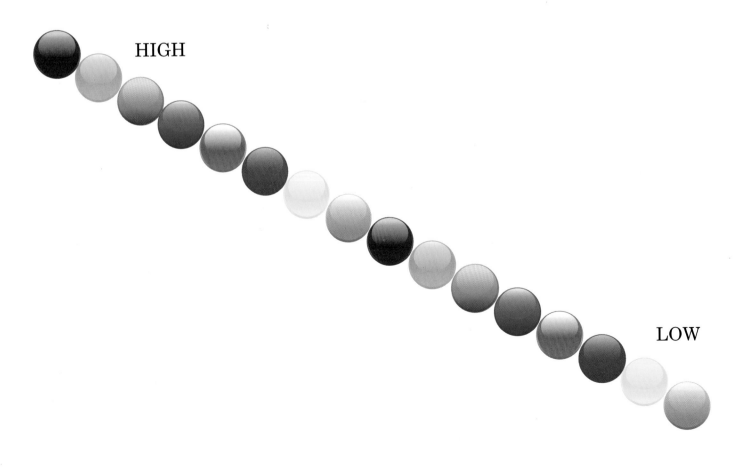

HIGH

LOW

The Music Alphabet

Different notes have different names. But they don't have names like "Sneezy," or "Grumpy." Notes have letter names. The *Music Alphabet* is easy because it uses only seven letters: A, B, C, D, E, F, and G.

Notes on paper are round. In this book, the letter name of each note is written in the middle of the circle. And to help you while you are first learning the note names, each note has its own color:

The Music Alphabet uses the same seven letters over and over again, from low to high, and backwards, from high to low.

HIGHER

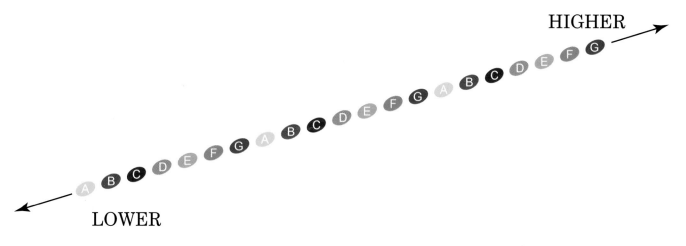

LOWER

Long and Short Notes

You already know that some notes sound high and some notes sound low. You also know that different notes have different letter names.

But maybe you didn't know that some notes sound long, and some notes sound short. Take a look at "Mary Had a Little Lamb" on the next page. Sing the first line: "Mary had a little lamb." When you sing the word "lamb" you hold it for a longer time than the words that came before it. "Lamb" has a note that is long. The notes before "lamb" are shorter.

Long notes are white Ⓔ ; short notes are black 🅔.
You can also tell how long a note is by looking at the colored bar above the note. The longer the colored bar, the longer the note.

Your First Song

"Mary Had a Little Lamb" is the first song in this book. Try singing it, and ask a grownup to help you if you need help.

If you look closely at the song, you'll see something that we haven't talked about yet. There are letters in boxes above the colored bars, like this: C, G. These are called *chord symbols*, and they are in the music for someone to play along with you on a guitar or a keyboard. If you know someone who can play along, the chord symbols are the part they should play. But even without the chords, you can still play and sing the songs!

Mary Had a Little Lamb

Words by Sarah Josepha Hale
Traditional Music

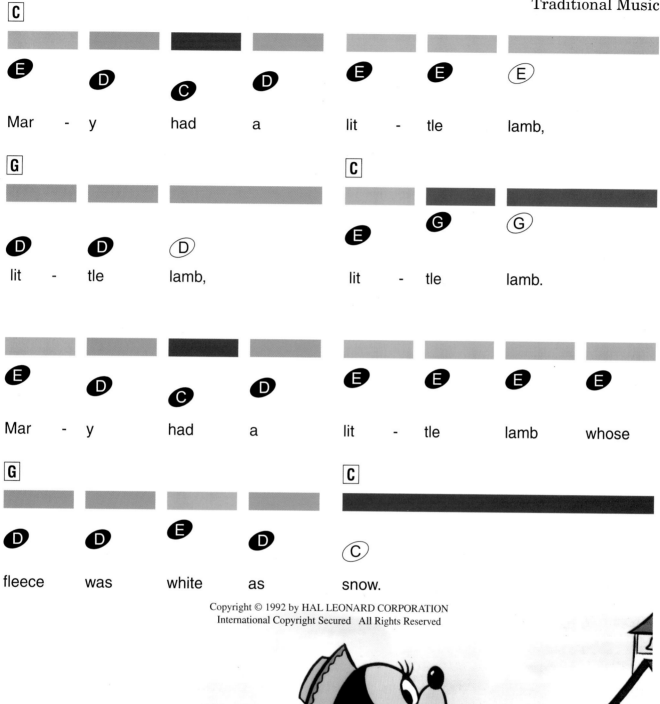

C

E   D   C   D   E   E   E

Mar - y   had   a   lit - tle   lamb,

G   **C**

D   D   D   E   G   G

lit - tle   lamb,   lit - tle   lamb.

E   D   C   D   E   E   E   E

Mar - y   had   a   lit - tle   lamb   whose

G   **C**

D   D   E   D   C

fleece   was   white   as   snow.

7

The Staff

To make it easier to see which notes are higher or lower than others, music notes are written on a set of five lines and four spaces called a *staff*. At the beginning of the staff is a *clef sign* to name the lines and spaces. The clef sign we will use is called the *Treble Clef*.

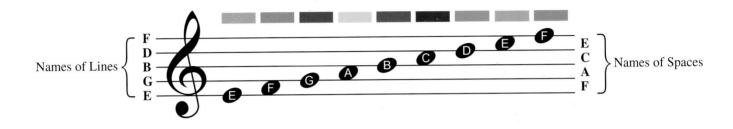

As you can see, each line and space on the staff has a letter name of its own. Each note on a particular line or in a particular space has the same name.

It's easy to remember the names of the lines and spaces. From bottom to the top the *lines* are: **E-G-B-D-F**. One way to remember this is to say, "**E**very **G**ood **B**oy **D**oes **F**ine."

From bottom to top the *spaces* are named **F-A-C-E**. This is easy to remember because the names of the spaces spell "face."

If a note is too high or too low to fit on the staff, extra lines can be added. These short lines are called *ledger lines*.

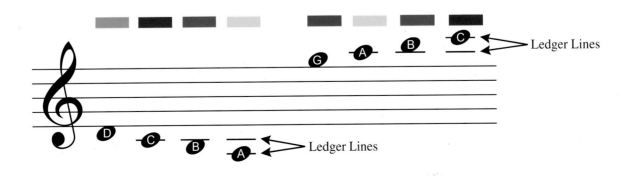

Notes on the Staff

These notes on the staff spell words. Place the notes on the correct line or space. The first one is done for you.

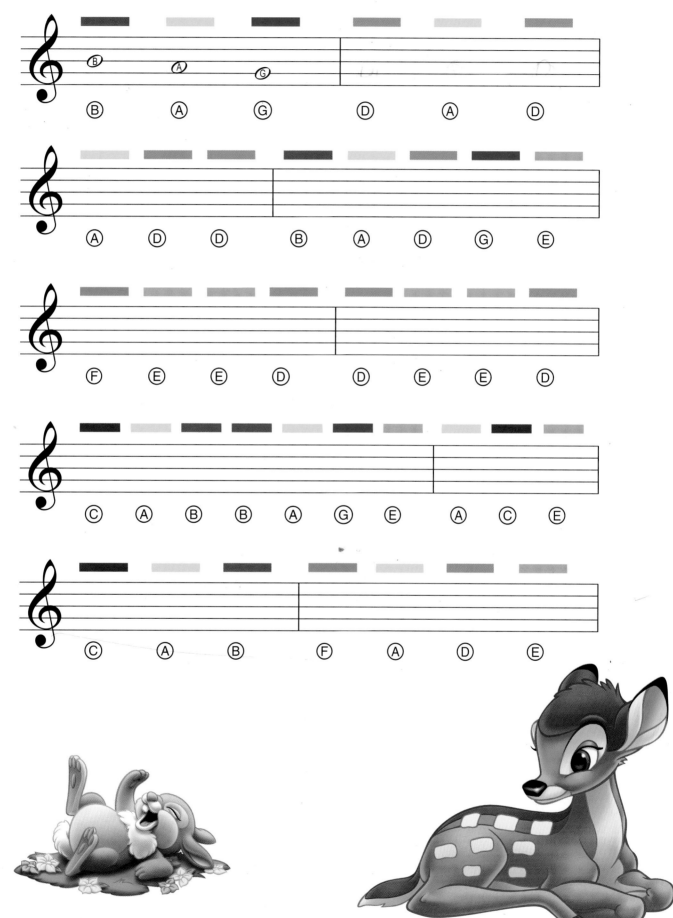

The Keyboard

It's easy to play notes on the piano keyboard. The keyboard is organized in groups of *black keys* and *white keys*. Take a look at the keyboard below to see the pattern of black key groups.

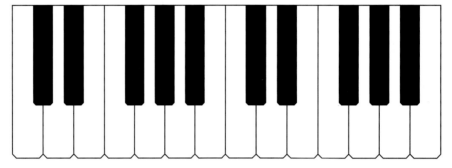

The white keys are named just like the notes on the staff, using the seven letters of the music alphabet.

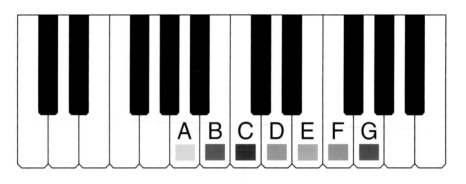

To help you learn the names of the white keys, we've included colored stickers for you to place on your keyboard. Carefully attach them using the directions found on the sticker sheet.

Finger numbers tell us which finger to use when we play notes on the keyboard. We number the fingers 1-5, and thumb is always number 1.

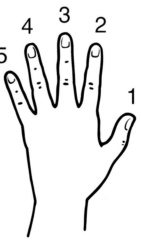
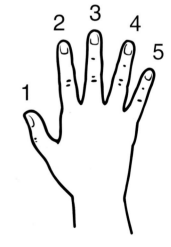

Left Hand (L.H.)   Right Hand (R.H.)

Name the Keys

Practice naming the white keys on the keyboards below.

Color all the Cs, Ds, and Es. These notes touch the groups of two black keys.

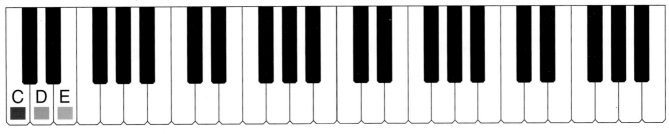

Color all the Fs, Gs, As, and Bs. These notes touch the groups of three black keys.

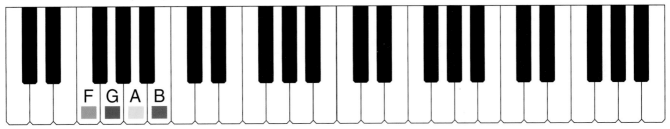

Fill in the names of the missing keys:

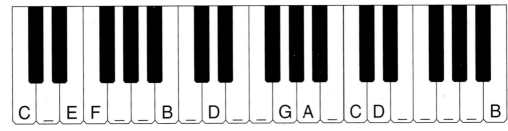

Use the finger numbers given to play white keys on your keyboard.

Use your right hand to play all the Cs on your keyboard with finger 2.
Use your left hand to play all the Gs on your keyboard with finger 3.
Use your right hand to play all the As with finger 4.
Use your right hand to play all the Ds with finger 3.
Use your left hand to play all the Es with finger 2.
Use your right hand to play the highest B with finger 5.
Use your left hand to play the lowest F with finger 1.

Play and Sing the Music Alphabet

Here are two songs to help you play and sing the music alphabet. Learn them well so we can dance to them! Sing the note names as you play.

Minnie's Dance

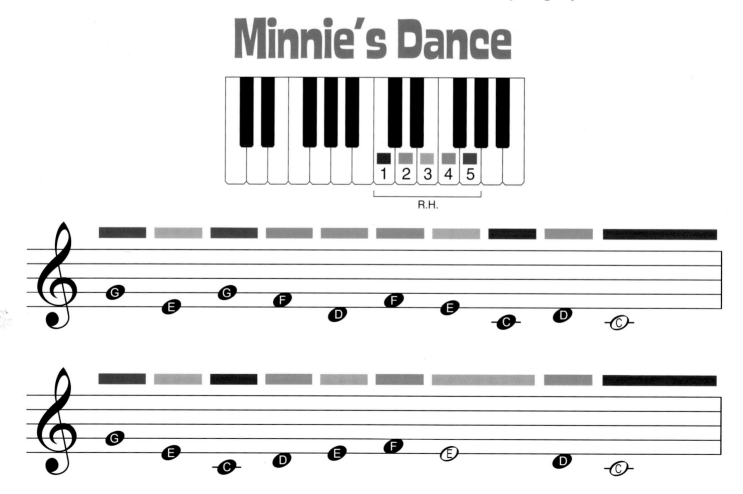

Use your left-hand thumb to help you play "Mickey, Row the Boat Ashore." The small keyboard shows you which fingers you will use.

Mickey, Row the Boat Ashore

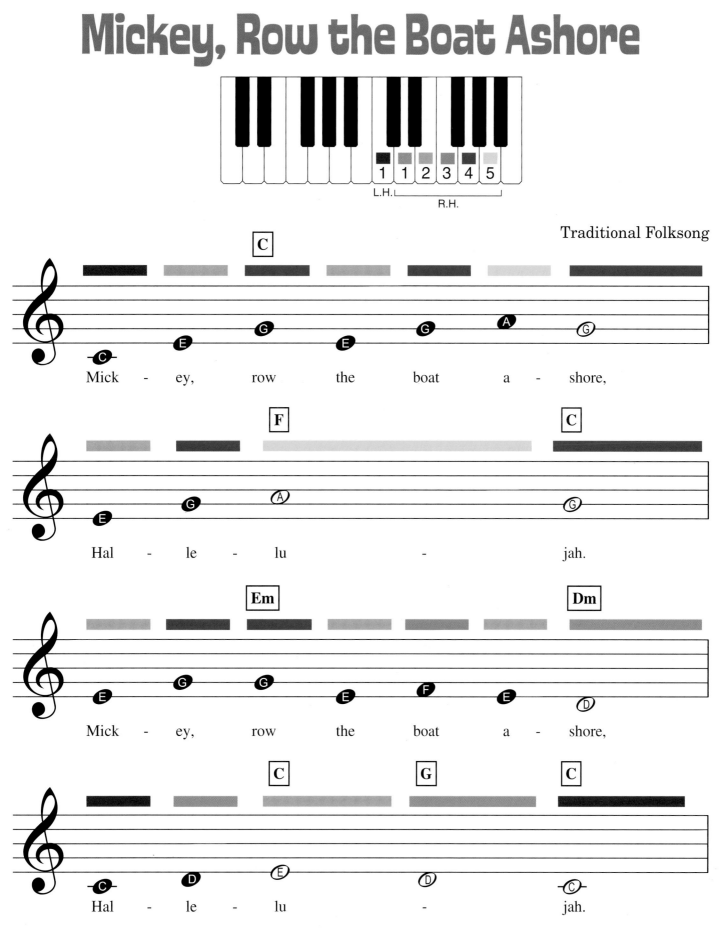

Traditional Folksong

Note Values

A music note tells us two things: how high or low a sound is, and how long the sound lasts.

You already know how high or low a note will sound by where it is on the staff. You also know that black notes are short, and white notes are long. But that isn't enough. We need to be more exact about how long the notes are.

Note values are measured in *beats*. When you tap your foot or clap your hands along with a song, you are tapping or clapping the *beat*.

The longest note value in most music is a *whole note*. The chart below shows how a whole note (and a pizza!) can be divided into smaller pieces of equal size.

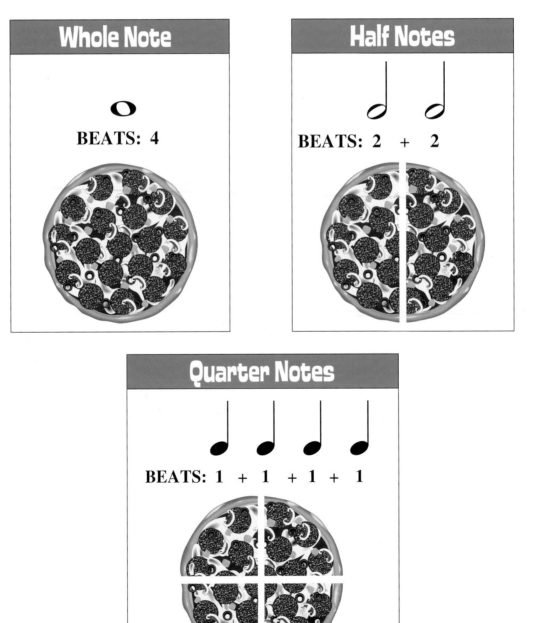

Coloring Fun

Use the note values to color Baloo. If the note equals four beats, color those areas green. If the note equals two beats, color those areas brown. If the note equals one beat, color the areas gray.

Connect the Dots

Can you name this symbol?

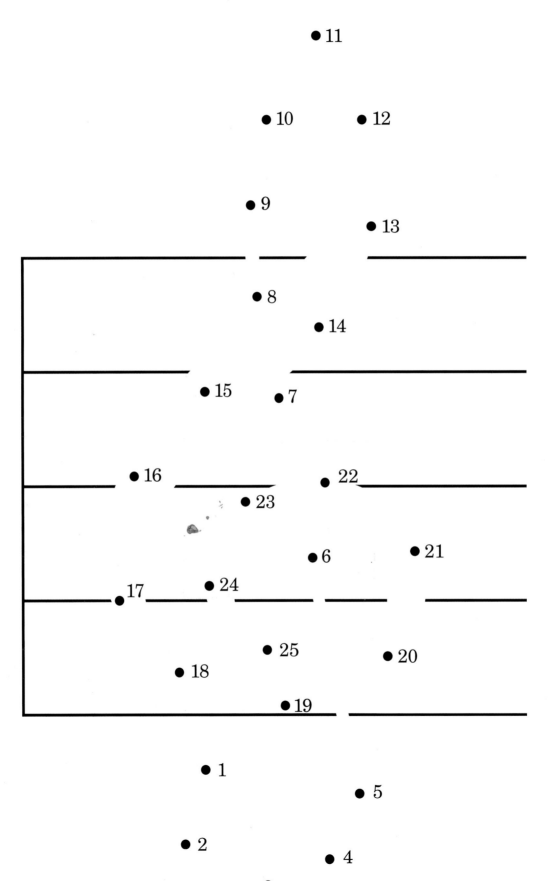

● 11

● 10   ● 12

● 9

● 13

● 8

● 14

● 15   ● 7

● 16   ● 22

● 23

● 6   ● 21

● 24

17

● 25   ● 20

● 18

● 19

● 1

● 5

● 2

● 4

● 3

What makes music fun is the way the seven letters of the music alphabet and the long and short notes get all mixed up together to make songs. Sometimes it quacks me up! (Hee-hee-hee!)

How Music Is Organized

You already know about the *staff*, which shows you how high or low the notes are. Here's the staff with some added music symbols to help you read the notes. You'll always find a *clef sign* at the beginning of the song. *Bar lines* divide the staff into *measures*, which contain groups of beats. Right next to the clef sign is a *time signature*. The top number tells you how many beats are in each measure. The 4 on the bottom reminds you that a quarter note equals one beat. There is a *double bar line* at the end of the staff. This sign tells you where the song ends.

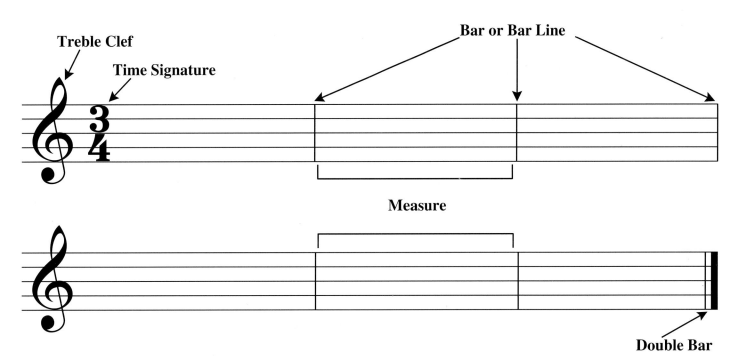

Counting Notes in 3/4 Time

Here's a new note, the dotted half note: ♩.

A dotted half note looks like a half note with an added dot.
This note equals three beats.

"Feed the Birds" has a 3/4 time signature. The number 3 on top tells us there are three beats in each measure. Tap your foot or count along with the numbers "1-2-3" for each measure to make sure that you keep a steady beat.

Feed the Birds
from Walt Disney's MARY POPPINS

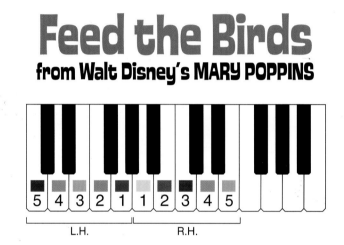

Words and Music by Richard M. Sherman
and Robert B. Sherman

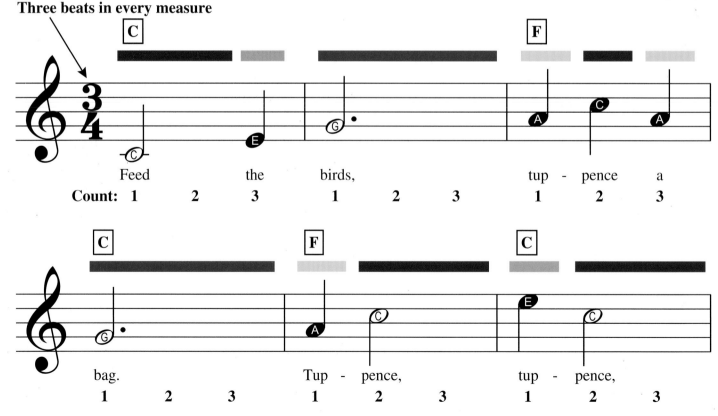

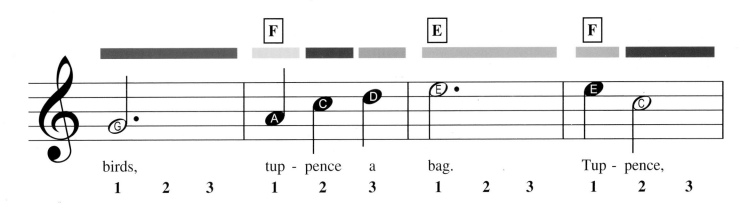

tup - pence a bag. Feed the

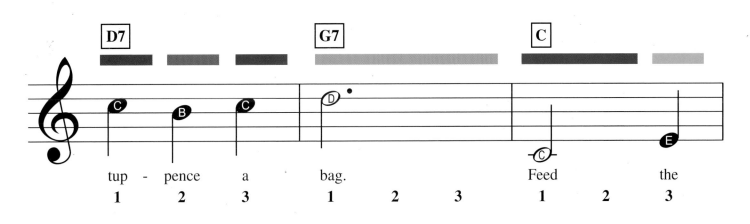

birds, tup - pence a bag. Tup - pence,

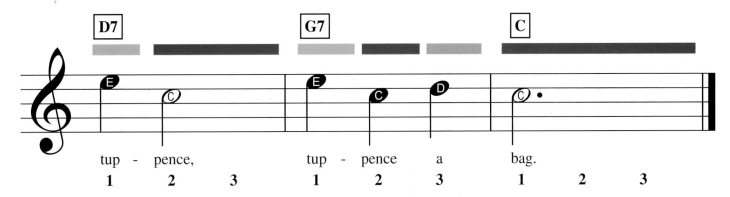

tup - pence, tup - pence a bag.

Counting Notes in $\frac{4}{4}$ Time

"Safety First" has a $\frac{4}{4}$ time signature. The number 4 on top tells us there are four beats in each measure. Tap or count along to make sure you keep four steady beats in each measure.

Safety First

Four beats in every measure

Words by Gil George
Music by Wanda Sykes

C		G

Safe - ty first,   safe - ty first, be
Count: 1   2   3   4   1   2   3   4

C		F

care - ful what you do.   Don - ald Duck,
1   2   3   4   1   2   3   4   1   2   3   4

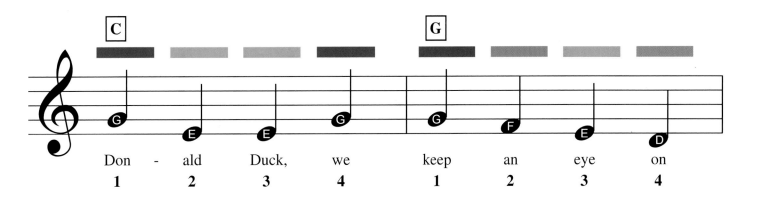

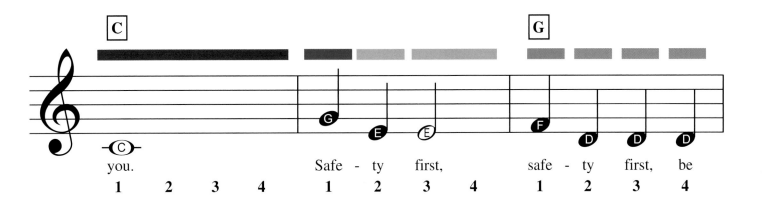

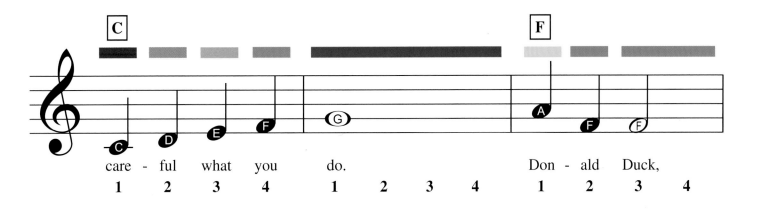

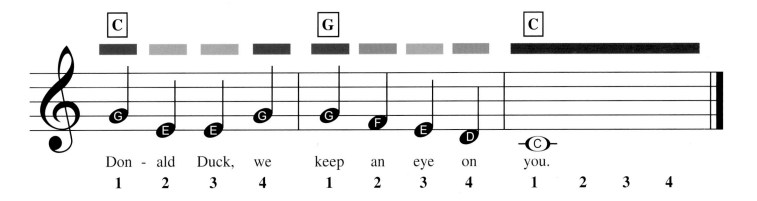

Add the Missing Bar Lines

You know that bar lines divide music into measures. And you know that the time signature tells us how many beats are in each measure. Our next song has four beats in each measure. Draw the bar lines where they are needed before you play "Supercalifragilisticexpialidocious." To check whether you've put the bar lines in the right places, see page 96.

Supercalifragilisticexpialidocious
from Walt Disney's MARY POPPINS

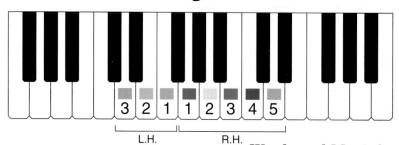

Words and Music by Richard M. Sherman
and Robert B. Sherman

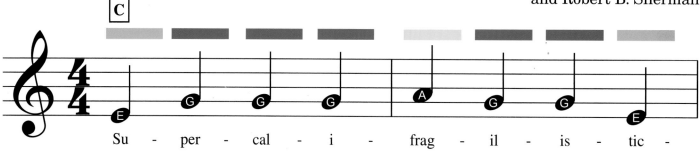

Su – per – cal – i – frag – il – is – tic –

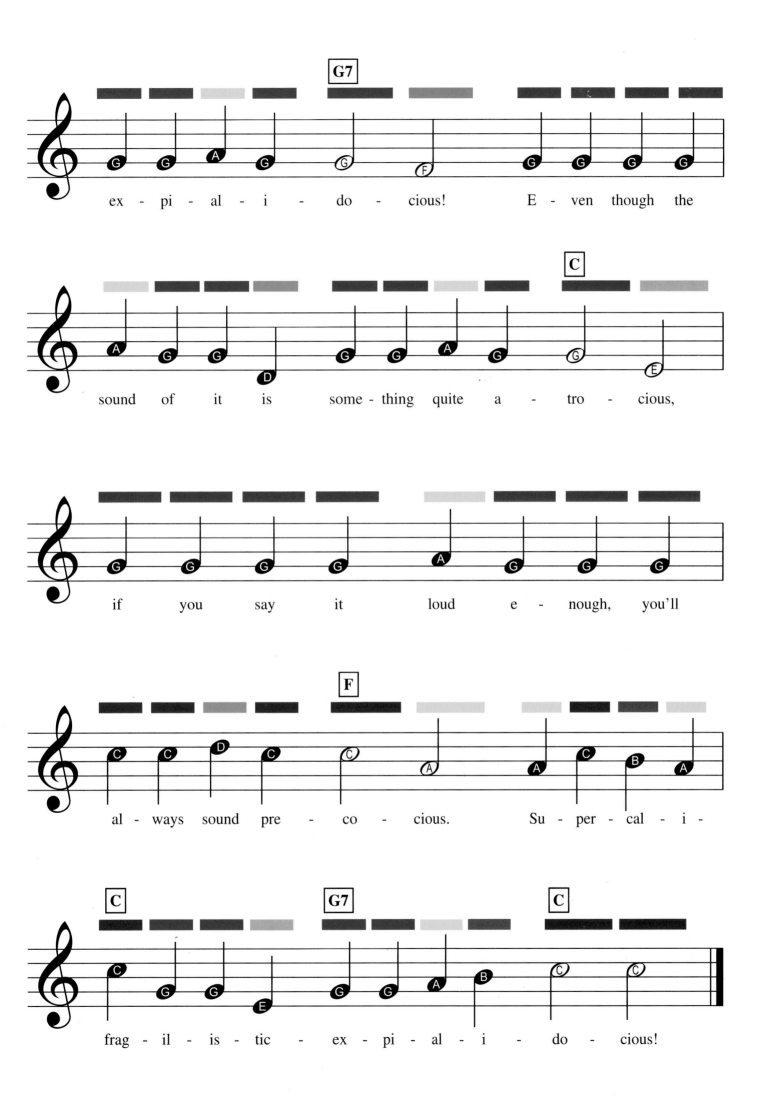

Rests

Rests are music symbols that stand for silence. A rest will tell you when **not** to play a note. Like notes, each rest is worth a certain number of beats, as shown below.

WHOLE REST	HALF REST	QUARTER REST
4 BEATS	2 BEATS	1 BEAT

Quarter rests and a half rest appear in our next song, "The Bare Necessities." When you come to the rest, count the beats until it's time to play the next melody note. Practice counting rests in the examples below.

The Bare Necessities

from Walt Disney's THE JUNGLE BOOK

Words and Music by Terry Gilkyson

Look for the bare ne - ces - si - ties, the
Look for the bare ne - ces - si - ties, the

Repeat Sign

A *Repeat Sign* is used at the end of "The Bare Necessities." This music symbol tells you to go back to the beginning of the song and play it again. When this happens, there is usually more than one set of words (*verses*) below the melody notes.

Crossword Fun

ACROSS

2. The bottom number of a time signature tells you what kind of note is one _____ long.

4. A _____ note lasts two beats.

6. You can divide a whole note into smaller pieces, just like a _____.

7. A treble _____ appears at the beginning of a song.

9. The same way you can put beads together to make a necklace, you can put _____ together to make music.

13. A whole note lasts _____ beats.

14. Black notes are short. White notes are _____.

15. The letter names of the spaces on the staff, from bottom to top, spell this word.

16. A _____ is the space between two bar lines.

18. The top number of a time signature tells you how many _____ are in a measure.

DOWN

1. Notes that are too high or too low to fit on the staff are written using ledger _____.

2. A double _____ tells you where the song ends.

3. In $\frac{3}{4}$ time there are _____ beats in every measure.

5. The letters in the music alphabet are: _____.

8. The _____ half note lasts for three beats.

10. White notes are long. Black notes are _____.

11. In $\frac{4}{4}$ time the _____ note is one beat long.

12. Notes are written on the _____, which has five lines.

17. There are _____ letters in the music alphabet.

Answers on page 96.

Note Reading Review

Name the notes and color Jiminy Cricket with crayons, pencils or markers using the note and color key at the bottom of the page.

| orange | green | dark blue | yellow | black | red | light blue |

Pick-up Notes

Your next song, "The Work Song," starts differently. Two melody notes are played before the first full measure. These are called *pick-up notes*. These pick-up notes are two quarter notes, or two beats. You may wonder where the other two beats in the measure are. Take a look at the end of the song. As you know, the half rest is worth two beats. The half rest plus the two quarter notes equal four beats—one full measure.

The Work Song
from Walt Disney's CINDERELLA

Words and Music by Mack David,
Al Hoffman and Jerry Livingston

Cin - der - el - la, Cin - der - el - la, all I

hear is Cin - der - el - la, from the mo - ment that I

Ties

Earlier in the book you learned that a whole note is our longest note, and that it lasts four beats. Then how do composers write longer notes? They use *ties*. Ties are curved lines that connect two or more of the same note name to make longer notes. The tied notes must be on the same line or in the same space. The first note is played or sung and held for the full value of all the tied notes. Play and count the example below.

G   4 + 2 = 6   G   2 + 1 = 3

1 2 3 4   1 2 3 4   1 2 3 4

1st and 2nd Endings

"It's a Small World" on page 32 uses the repeat sign in a different way. Sometimes a whole section of music can be repeated, ending in a slightly different way the second time. This is indicated by *1st and 2nd ending* signs. Play from the beginning to the repeat sign at the end of the song. The measures leading up to the repeat sign are marked with a first ending sign. Now go back to the first repeat sign. Play the second verse, and when you get to the end, skip the first ending and play the second ending measures. 1st and 2nd ending signs look like this:

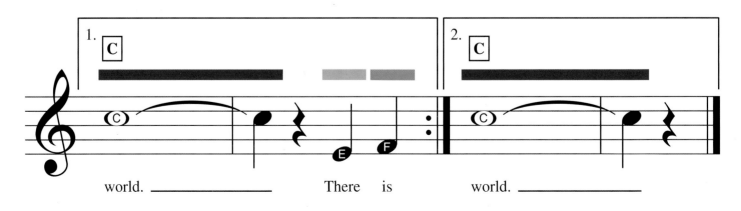

1. C   2. C

C   C

world. _____   There is   world. _____

Music Math

Let's do some music math! Add the values of the tied notes to find the answer to each of these musical equations. The first one is done for you. Check your answers on page 96.

1.

__2__ + __1__ = __3__

2.

___ + ___ + ___ = ___

3.

___ + ___ = ___

4.

___ + ___ + ___ = ___

5.

___ + ___ = ___

6.

___ + ___ = ___

7.

___ + ___ + ___ = ___

8.

___ + ___ = ___

9.

___ + ___ + ___ + ___ = ___

10.

___ + ___ + ___ + ___ = ___

It's a Small World
from Disneyland Resort® and Magic Kingdom® Park

Words and Music by Richard M. Sherman
and Robert B. Sherman

Steps and Skips

When notes on the staff move from a space to a line, or a line to a space, we can describe that distance as a *step*.

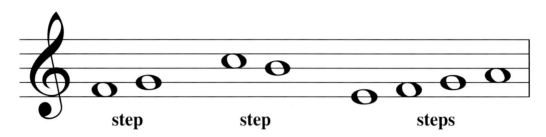

step   **step**   **steps**

On the keyboard, a step is the distance from one key to the very next key. Steps can move up or down.

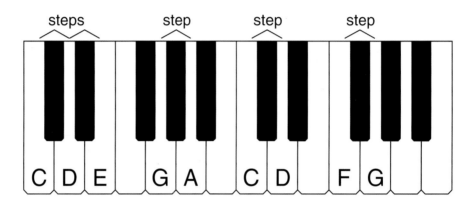

When notes are written from one line to the next line, or from a space to the next space, we call that distance a *skip*.

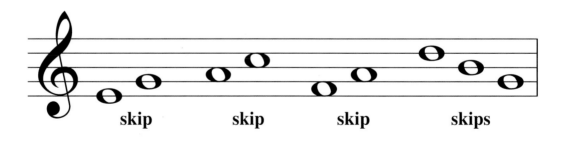

skip   **skip**   **skip**   **skips**

On the keyboard, we skip a white key when we skip a line or space on the staff. We can skip up or down.

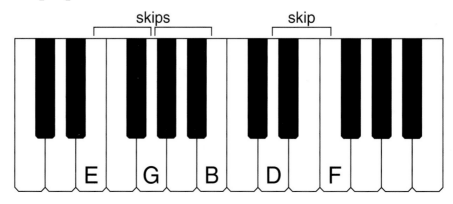

On the keyboards below, write in the note names to show steps or skips.

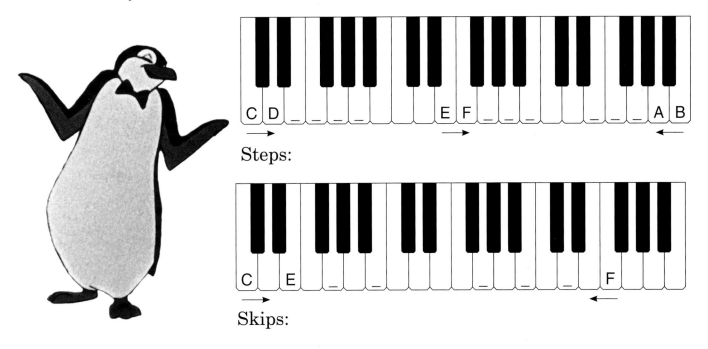

Steps:

Skips:

On the staff below, label the notes as steps or skips.
The first example is done for you.

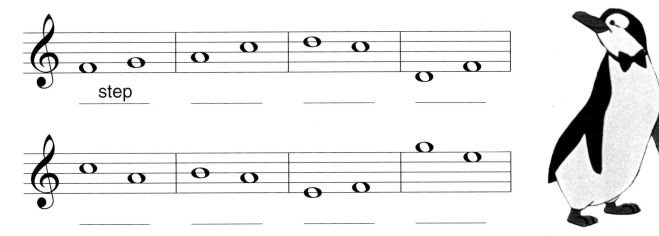

step

In each measure below, draw notes that step or skip.

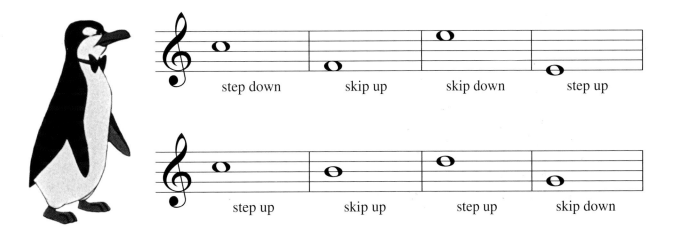

step down   skip up   skip down   step up

step up   skip up   step up   skip down

Answers on page 96.

A *scale* is a pattern of notes that step. An *arpeggio* is a pattern of notes that skip. Take a look at the notes that step and skip in "Scales and Arpeggios." Knowing if the notes step or skip makes a song easier to play.

Scales and Arpeggios

from Walt Disney's THE ARISTOCATS

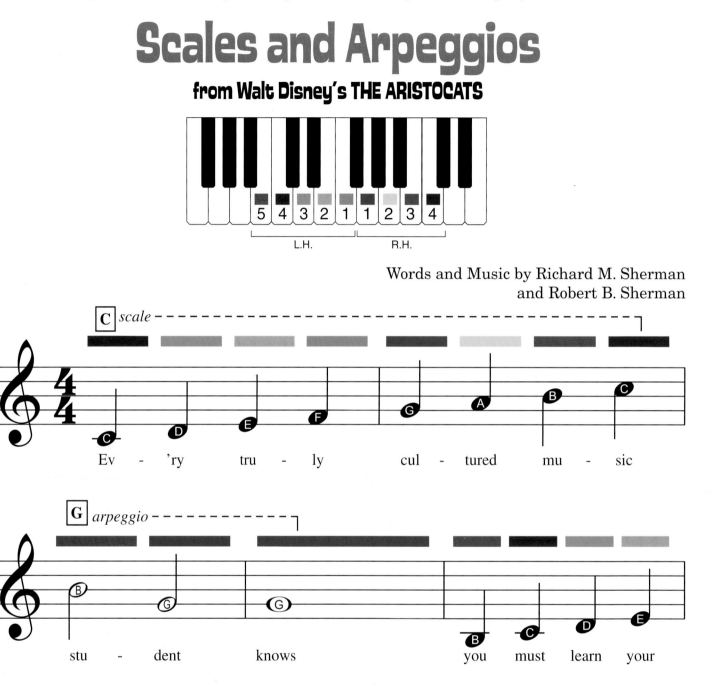

Words and Music by Richard M. Sherman
and Robert B. Sherman

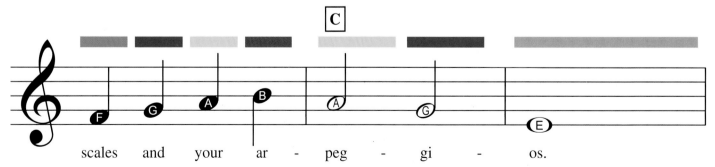

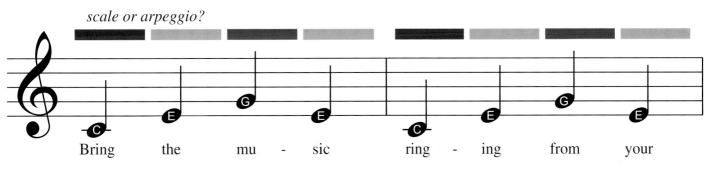

scale or arpeggio?

Bring the mu – sic ring – ing from your

F   C *scale or arpeggio?*

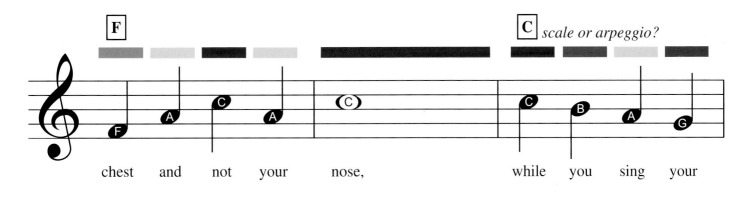

chest and not your nose,   while you sing your

G   C

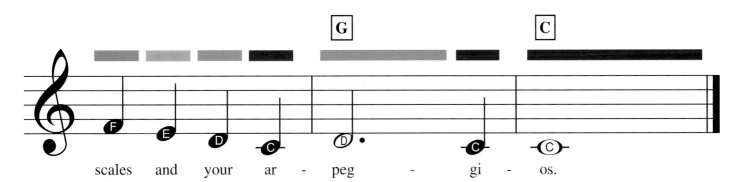

scales and your ar – peg – gi – os.

37

Eighth Notes

Music uses many different kinds of notes. So far, you've learned about quarter notes, half notes, dotted half notes, and whole notes. Here's something new: eighth notes!

One eighth note looks like a quarter note with a flag. When two or more eighth notes appear together, the flags turn into beams. When the time signature is $\frac{4}{4}$ eighth notes are often connected in groups of two or four. The beams make reading the eighth notes easier.

Practice drawing some flags and beams.
The first example in each line is done for you.

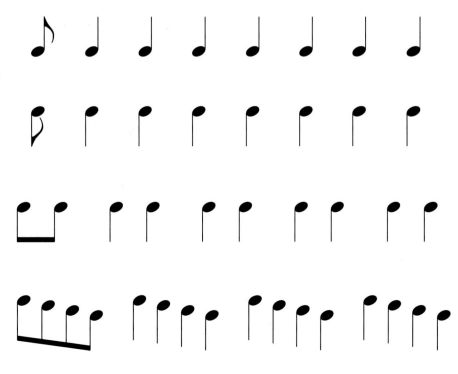

38

Counting Eighth Notes

Remember when we used a pizza to show the value of notes? One whole pizza was like a whole note. When we cut the pizza in half, we could see two half notes. Then we divided each half into quarters. If we divide the pizza one more time, we'll divide the four quarter notes into eight eighth notes. We'll also have eight pieces of pizza.

When you count eighth notes and half beats, it's easier if you think about tapping your foot to the music. Look at Goofy's shoe, tapping along with the quarter notes. We count the quarter notes 1-2-3-4.

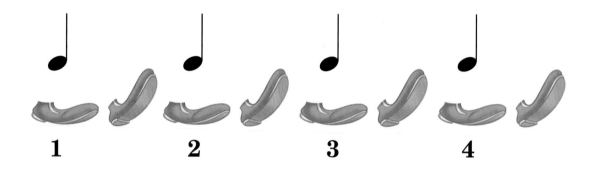

1   **2**   **3**   **4**

As he taps, his foot moves up and down, tapping on the floor for each quarter note beat. To count eighth notes, he taps the same way but the notes sound twice as fast. Two eighth notes equal one quarter note.

Count: 1 & 2 & 3 & 4 &

The "ands" are when he raises his foot.

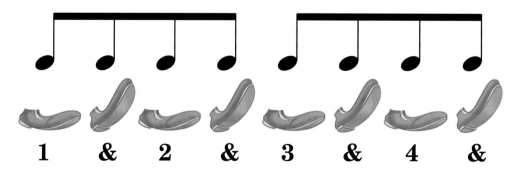

1   **&**   **2**   **&**   **3**   **&**   **4**   **&**

Try it yourself, tapping your foot and counting 1 & 2 & 3 & 4 &

Here are some rhythms to practice.
Don't forget to count and tap your foot.

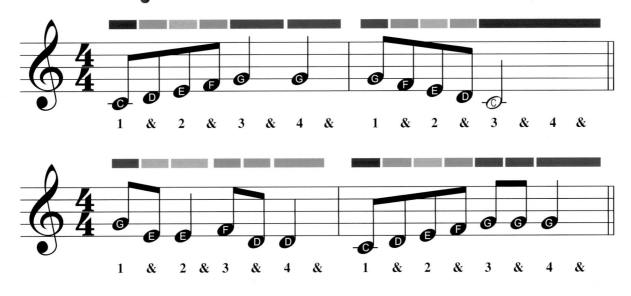

Eighth Rests

You know what rests are: symbols for silence, or places you don't play any notes.
An eighth rest lasts as long as an eighth note: half a beat. It looks like this:

Practice clapping and counting some rhythms with eighth rests.

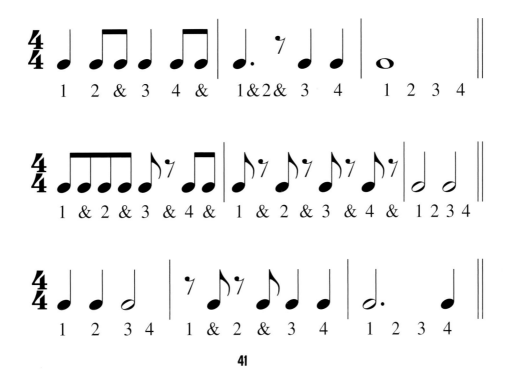

"Colors of the Wind" will give you a good chance to practice playing eighth notes. Tap your foot and sing the words to practice the rhythm before you play the notes on the keyboard. Notice you start with a pick-up note, and have a 1st and 2nd ending.

Colors of the Wind
from Walt Disney's POCAHONTAS

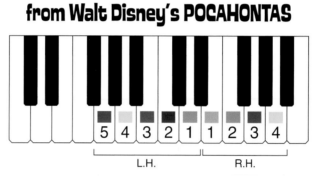

Music by Alan Menken
Lyrics by Stephen Schwartz

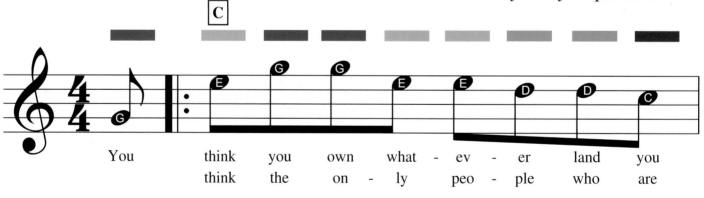

You think you own what-ev-er land you
think the on-ly peo-ple who are

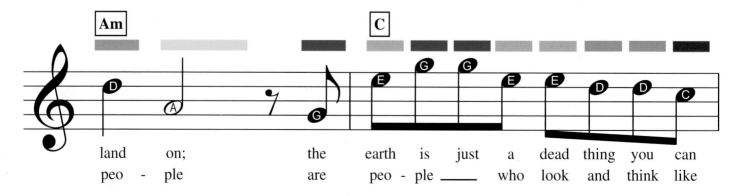

land on; the earth is just a dead thing you can
peo-ple are peo-ple _____ who look and think like

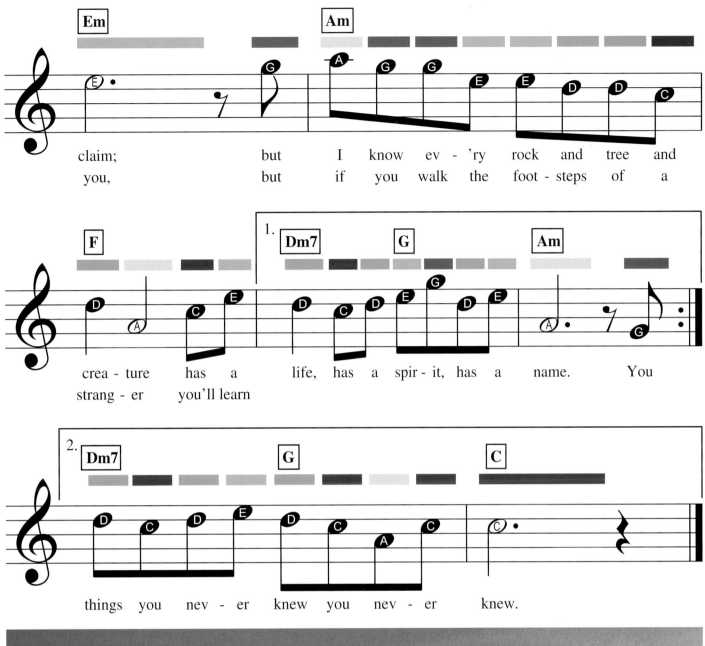

claim;   but   I   know   ev - 'ry   rock   and   tree   and
you,   but   if   you   walk   the   foot - steps   of   a

crea - ture   has   a   life, has a spir - it, has a   name.   You
strang - er   you'll learn

things   you   nev - er   knew   you   nev - er   knew.

Can you find the skips in this song? Remember, skips are notes that are written on the staff from a line to a line, or a space to a space. Knowing where the skips are will help you play this song. Keep the quarter notes steady, and the eighth notes smooth. Remember, eighth notes are twice as fast as quarter notes.

Never Smile at a Crocodile

from Walt Disney's PETER PAN

Words by Jack Lawrence
Music by Frank Churchill

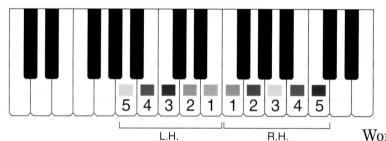

Nev - er smile at a croc - o - dile, no, you

can't get friend-ly with a croc - o - dile. Don't be tak - en in by his

Take a look at the keyboard below to see which fingers will play the keys. Left-hand finger 5 is marked on two keys. G has finger 5 marked in parenthesis. This means that you will move your left-hand finger down slightly (just one key) to play that G, returning your left-hand finger 5 to the A immediately after playing the G. We've marked those places in the music for you. After you've tried it a few times, it will become very easy to do!

Happy Working Song

from Walt Disney Pictures' ENCHANTED

Music by Alan Menken
Lyrics by Stephen Schwartz

| C | | | G/B | | F/A | | C/G |

Come, my lit - tle friends, as we all sing a hap - py lit - tle

| F | | C/E | | | G7/D | G |

work - ing song, mer - ry lit - tle voic - es clear and strong.

47

Mickey's Mixed-up Melody

Mickey would like you to fill in the missing measures so he can sing "Lavender Blue." The missing measures are all scrambled up. Decide which measures go in the empty spots, and copy them in. To check your work, sing or play the song. If you need some extra help, turn to page 96 for the answers.

Lavender Blue
(Dilly Dilly)
from Walt Disney's SO DEAR TO MY HEART

Words by Larry Morey
Music by Eliot Daniel

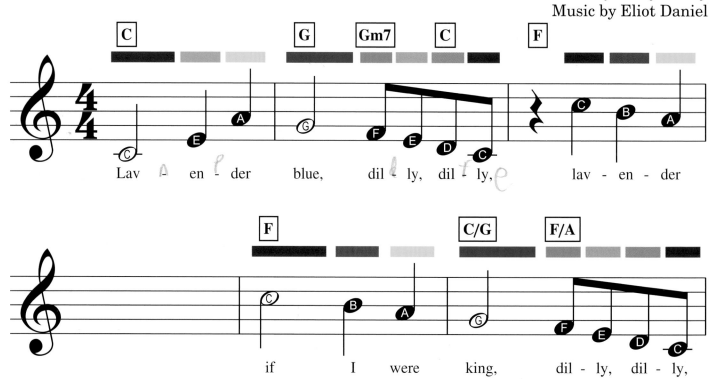

queen.

so,   dil - ly, dil - ly,   so?

I   told my -   I   told   me

Missing Measures:

Who   told   me

who   told   me

so.

green;

self,   dil - ly, dil - ly,

I'd   need   a

Dotted Notes

You know that a dotted half note equals three beats. The dot adds half the value of the note it follows. It's kind of like playing a tied note without the tie.

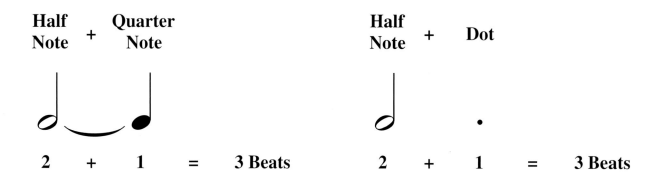

Half Note	+	Quarter Note		Half Note	+	Dot
2	+	1	= 3 Beats	2	+ 1	= 3 Beats

You can add a dot to any note to increase its value. When you add a dot to a quarter note, you add half a beat.

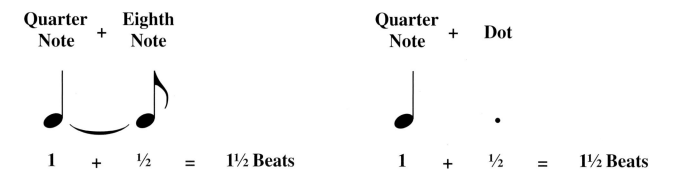

Quarter Note	+	Eighth Note		Quarter Note	+	Dot
1	+	½	= 1½ Beats	1	+ ½	= 1½ Beats

A dotted quarter note is often followed by an eighth note. Here are some dotted note rhythms to practice. Clap and count. You may wish to tap your foot to keep the beat.

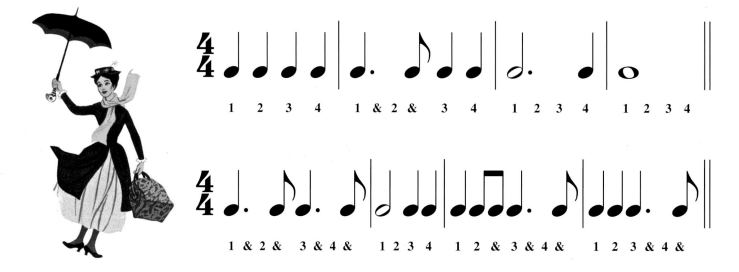

"Step in Time" is sung by Bert, the chimney sweep in *Mary Poppins*. Tap your foot to keep a strong beat as you count the dotted quarter note rhythms.

Step in Time
from Walt Disney's MARY POPPINS

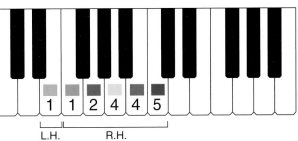

Words and Music by Richard M. Sherman
and Robert B. Sherman

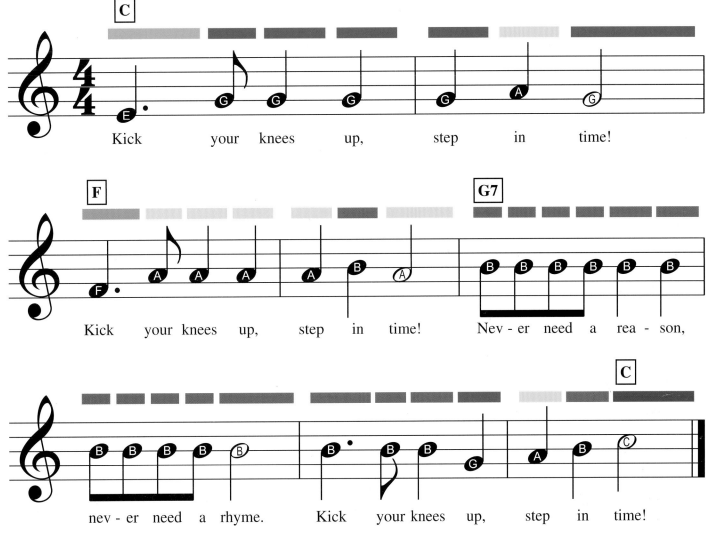

Look for dotted notes and tied notes in "A Whole New World." Clap and sing the words to help you feel the rhythm of the dotted notes. The 1st ending repeat takes you back to the beginning of the song. After the repeat, remember to skip the 1st ending and play the 2nd ending instead, continuing through to the end of the song.

A Whole New World
from Walt Disney's ALADDIN

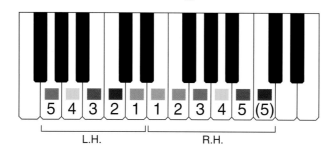

Music by Alan Menken
Lyrics by Tim Rice

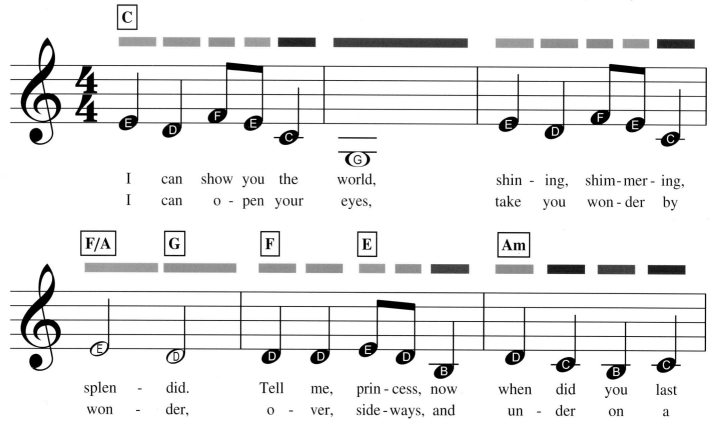

53

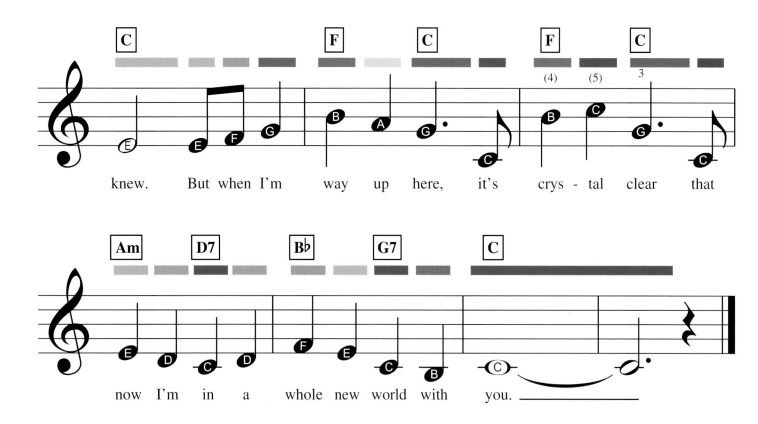

knew.   But when I'm   way up here,   it's   crys - tal   clear   that

now I'm in a whole new world with   you. _____

Note Matching

Draw a line from the note on the left to the pizza on the right that represents the same number of beats. The answers are on page 96.

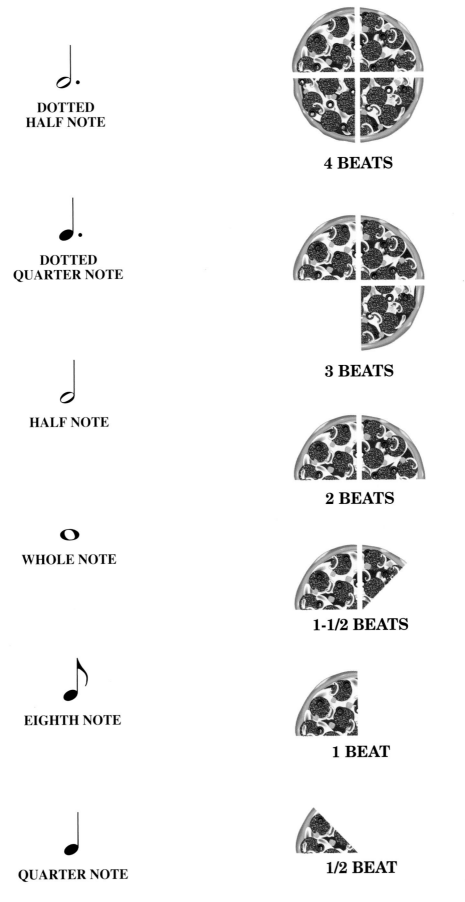

DOTTED
HALF NOTE

4 BEATS

DOTTED
QUARTER NOTE

3 BEATS

HALF NOTE

2 BEATS

WHOLE NOTE

1-1/2 BEATS

EIGHTH NOTE

1 BEAT

QUARTER NOTE

1/2 BEAT

Can you find the dotted quarter note in "True Love's Kiss?" Notice that left-hand finger 5 moves down to play the A three times in this song. The finger number is shown in parenthesis (5) to remind you. Move your left-hand finger 5 back to the B after playing the A each time.

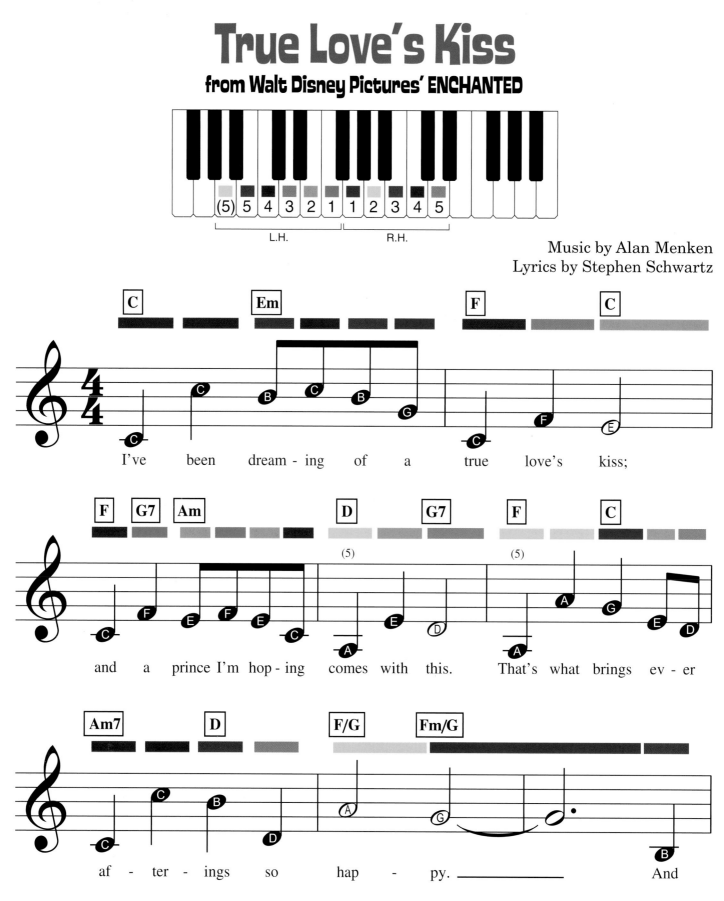

True Love's Kiss
from Walt Disney Pictures' ENCHANTED

Music by Alan Menken
Lyrics by Stephen Schwartz

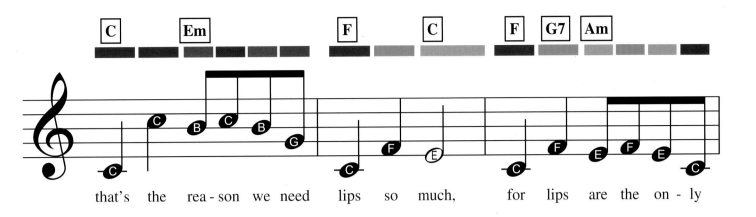

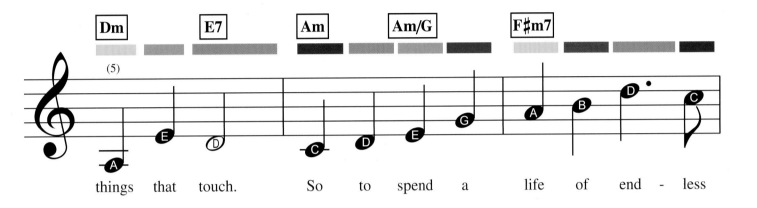

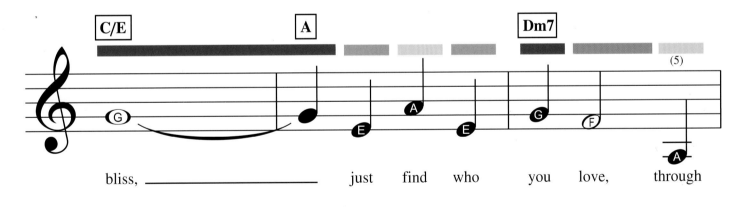

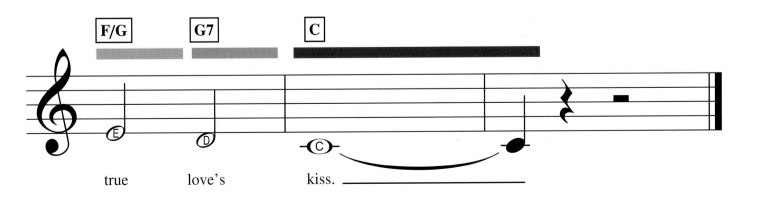

A New Time Signature: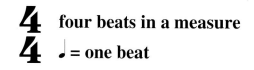

Earlier in this book, you learned that the top number of a time signature tells you how many beats are in each measure of a song, and that the bottom number of a time signature tells you what kind of note gets one beat.

For example, when the time signature is $\frac{4}{4}$, there are four beats in a measure, and the quarter note gets one beat.

4 four beats in a measure
4 ♩ = one beat

The next song, "Bibbidi-Bobbidi-Boo" has a new time signature: $\frac{6}{8}$. In this song, there are six beats in a measure, and now the eighth note will get one beat.

Count: 1   2   3   4   5   6

6 six beats in a measure
8 ♪ = one beat

I thought an eighth note is half a beat long. Now you say an eighth note gets one beat. I'm confused! Which is it?

The answer to Suzy's question is, "both." An eighth note can be half a beat long whenever the bottom number in the time signature is 4. *But in $\frac{6}{8}$ time, the eighth note gets one beat. Not only that, but in $\frac{6}{8}$ time a quarter note gets two beats.* One thing never changes—two eighth notes always equal one quarter note.

Here are some rhythms that appear in "Bibbidi-Bobbidi-Boo." Practice clapping and counting each of these examples. In $\frac{6}{8}$ time, the eighth notes are often beamed in groups of three.

Bibbidi-Bobbidi-Boo
(The Magic Song)
from Walt Disney's CINDERELLA

Words by Jerry Livingston
Music by Mack David
and Al Hoffman

Sa - la - ga - doo - la men - chick - a boo - la
Sa - la - ga - doo - la men - chick - a boo - la

Count: 1 2 3 4 5 6 1 2 3 4 5 6

bib - bi - di - bob - bi - di - boo. Put 'em to - geth - er and
bib - bi - di - bob - bi - di - boo. It - 'll do mag - ic, be -

what have you got? Bib - bi - di - bob - bi - di - boo.
lieve it or not. Bib - bi - di - bob - bi - di - boo.

Sa - la - ga - doo - la means men - chick - a boo - la -

60

Buzz & Woody's Time Signature Challenge

When the time signature is $\frac{4}{4}$, the quarter note equals 1 beat. Add the values of these notes in $\frac{4}{4}$ time. The first example is done for you.

When the time signature is $\frac{6}{8}$, the eighth note gets one beat. Add the values of these notes in $\frac{6}{8}$ time.

1. $\frac{4}{4}$ ♩ + ♩ = __2__ beats

1. $\frac{6}{8}$ ♪ + ♪ = __2__ beats

2. $\frac{4}{4}$ ♩ + ♩ = ___ beats

2. $\frac{6}{8}$ ♩ + ♪ = ___ beats

3. $\frac{4}{4}$ ♩ + ♩ = ___ beats

3. $\frac{6}{8}$ ♩. + ♩. = ___ beats

4. $\frac{4}{4}$ ♩ + 𝅝 = ___ beats

4. $\frac{6}{8}$ ♪♪♪ + ♩ = ___ beats

5. $\frac{4}{4}$ ♩ + ♩ + ♩ = ___ beats

5. $\frac{6}{8}$ ♩ + ♩ = ___ beats

6. $\frac{4}{4}$ ♩ + ♩. + ♩ = ___ beats

6. $\frac{6}{8}$ ♪ + ♩ + ♪ = ___ beats

Answers on page 96.

Counting in $\frac{6}{8}$ Time

We've been counting six beats per measure when we see the $\frac{6}{8}$ time signature. This works well when the *tempo* (speed) is slow or medium. When a fast song is written in $\frac{6}{8}$ time, we can hear the music as having a feeling of two strong beats per measure. You may wish to count two beats, instead of six. Take a look at the rhythms below.

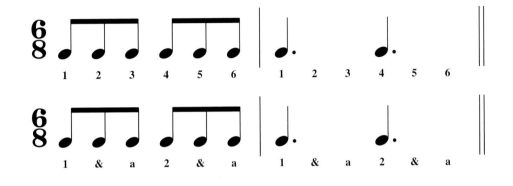

Our next song, "Mickey Mouse March," is a fast song written with a $\frac{6}{8}$ time signature. There are a lot of quarter notes followed by eighth notes. This long-short rhythm may remind you of a galloping horse. Try clapping this rhythm both ways: with six beats per measure, and with a feeling of two beats per measure.

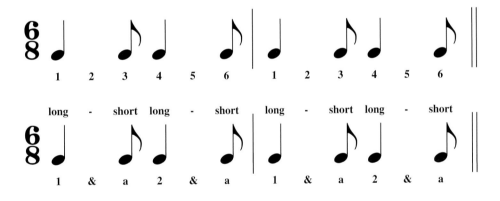

Try the first phrase of "Mickey Mouse March" counted in two. Say the words and clap the notes.

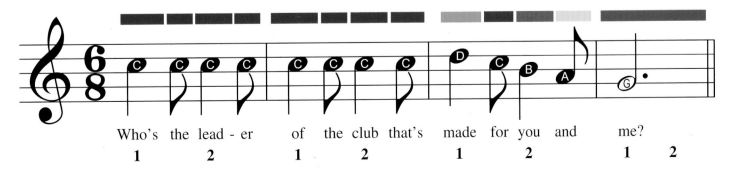

Count this march with a feeling of two beats per measure. Look ahead for the repeat sign, and look out for the second ending after the repeat.

Mickey Mouse March

from Walt Disney's THE MICKEY MOUSE CLUB

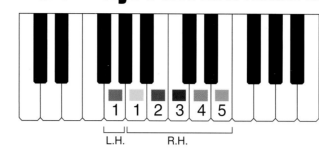

Words and Music by Jimmie Dodd

C **Am**

Who's the lead - er of the club that's
Hey, there! Hi, there! Ho, there! You're as

D7 **G7** **C** **C7**

made for you and me?
wel - come as can be!

M - I - C -

F **Fm** **C** **G7** 1. **C** **G7**

K - E - Y   M - O - U - S - E!

2. **C** **F**

E!   Mick - ey   Mouse! _____   Mick - ey

Sharps

You know the seven letters of the music alphabet pretty well by now. You're ready to learn some new notes. One way to show some of these notes is with a *sharp sign*, which looks like this: ♯

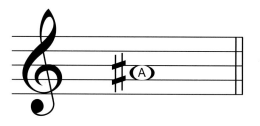

The name of this note is not A anymore—it's *A sharp* (A♯).

A note with a sharp in front of it sounds a half step higher than it would without the sharp. A *half step* is a very small distance in music. On a keyboard, we describe it as one key to the **very next** key—often a white key to black key.

Sharped notes are usually between two musical letter names. For example, A♯ is between A and B. This is easiest to see on the keyboard, where sharped notes are usually black keys.

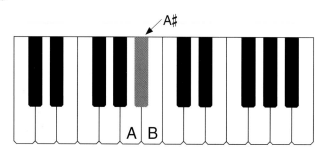

Remember, when you see a sharp in front of a note, play or sing a half step higher. A note with a sharp sounds a little higher than the same note without a sharp.

Sharps in the Forest

Draw a line connecting the sharped notes on the staff to the notes on the keyboards below. Check your answers on page 96.

There is one sharped note in "Let's Go Fly a Kite." Can you find it? Play this F♯ with finger 2 on the black key. It's marked for you on the small keyboard above the song.

Let's Go Fly a Kite
from Walt Disney's MARY POPPINS

Words and Music by Richard M. Sherman
and Robert B. Sherman

F
Let's go fly a

C
kite up to the high - est

G7
height! Let's go fly a

C
kite and send it soar -

Flats

In our next song, "Chim Chim Cher-ee," you'll see a note with a flat in front of it, like this:

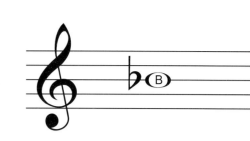

A note with a flat in front of it is a half step *lower* than it would be without the flat.

The flat is added to the name of the note. In this example, the name of the note is not B anymore, it's **B-flat**, also written: **B♭**

Just like sharps, flat notes usually fall between two letter name notes. For example, B♭ is between A and B. On keyboard instruments, flat notes are usually black keys.

Wait a minute! Before you said that A♯ is between A and B. Now you're saying that B♭ is between A and B! Are you trying to get me mixed up?

No, we're not trying to get the alien mixed up. That black key between A and B can be called either sharp or flat. Check out the keyboard below. The black keys get their name from the white keys. When going *up* the scale, the black keys have "sharp" names. When going *down* the scale, the black keys have "flat" names.

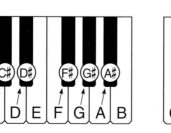 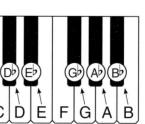

Just remember, when you see a **flat** in front of a note, play the very next note **lower** on the keyboard. When you see a **sharp** in front of a note, play the very next note **higher** on the keyboard.

Sharp or Flat?

Placing a sharp in front of a note raises the pitch a half step. Add sharps to these notes. Be sure to place the sharp sign in front of the note. The "center square" of the sharp sign includes the line or space of the note.

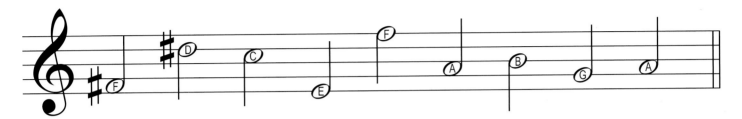

Placing a flat in front of a note lowers the pitch a half step. Add flat signs to these notes. Place the round part of the flat sign carefully to include the line or space of the note.

Name the following sharp and flat notes.

1. ____   2. ____   3. ____   4. ____   5. ____

6. ____   7. ____   8. ____   9. ____   10. ____

Answers on page 96.

D.C. al Fine

A new kind of repeat is used in "Chim Chim Cher-ee." After you take the second ending, there is the direction, *D.C. al Fine*. These are Italian words pronounced *D.C. al FEE-nay*. (Lots of musical terms are in Italian. We'll be learning a few more later.) D. C. stands for *Da Capo*, which means to go back to the beginning of the song, and *al Fine* means to play to where the word *Fine* is, and end the song there. *Fine* means finish, or end. Sing through "Chim Chim Cher-ee" to practice following the repeat sign and D.C al Fine.

Dynamics

Dynamics are symbols for how softly or loudly the music should sound. Most of the words are in Italian. Here are some common dynamics, and what they mean.

*piano **p*** = soft

*mezzo piano **mp*** = medium soft

*forte **f*** = loud

*mezzo forte **mf*** = medium loud

There are other symbols in music that help you play expressively. One of those symbols is *rit.*, which is short for *ritardando*, meaning to slow the music slightly. You'll often see this at the end of a song, like in "Can You Feel the Love Tonight." Slow the music slightly to bring the song to a gentle ending.

There are three black keys in "Chim Chim Cher-ee." Can you find them in the music? You might circle them so they are easier to see. The keyboard will show you which fingers play the sharps and flats. Just take it slow your first time through and you will see how fun it is to play the black keys!

Chim Chim Cher-ee
from Walt Disney's MARY POPPINS

Words and Music by Richard M. Sherman
and Robert B. Sherman

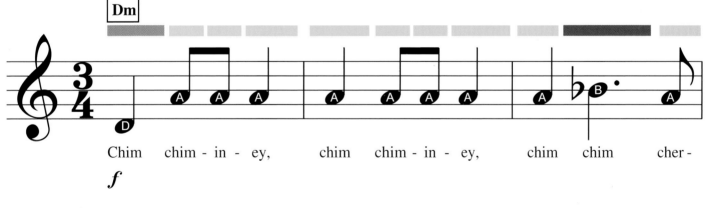

Chim   chim - in - ey,   chim   chim - in - ey,   chim   chim   cher-

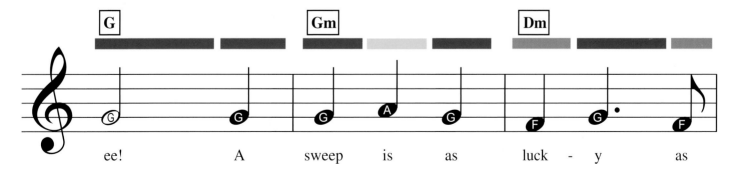

ee!   A   sweep   is   as   luck - y   as

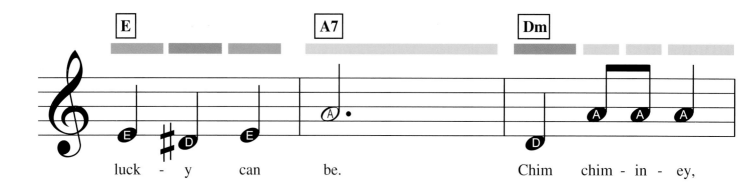

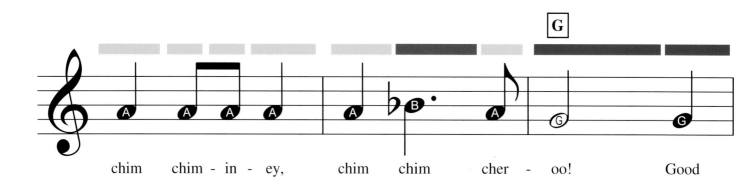

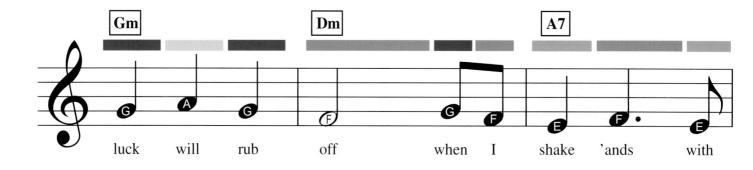

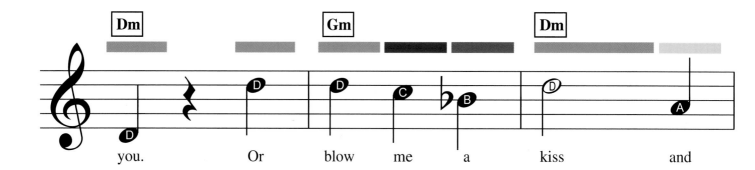

Can You Feel the Love Tonight

from Walt Disney Pictures' THE LION KING

The tempo marking tells us about the speed and character of a song.

Music by Elton John
Lyrics by Tim Rice

Moderately slow Ballad

D.C. al Coda is another way to write a repeating section of music. After you go back to the beginning (D.C.) play until you see the direction "To Coda," then jump ahead to the section marked "Coda" to finish the song.

Beauty and the Beast

from Walt Disney's BEAUTY AND THE BEAST

Lyrics by Howard Ashman
Music by Alan Menken

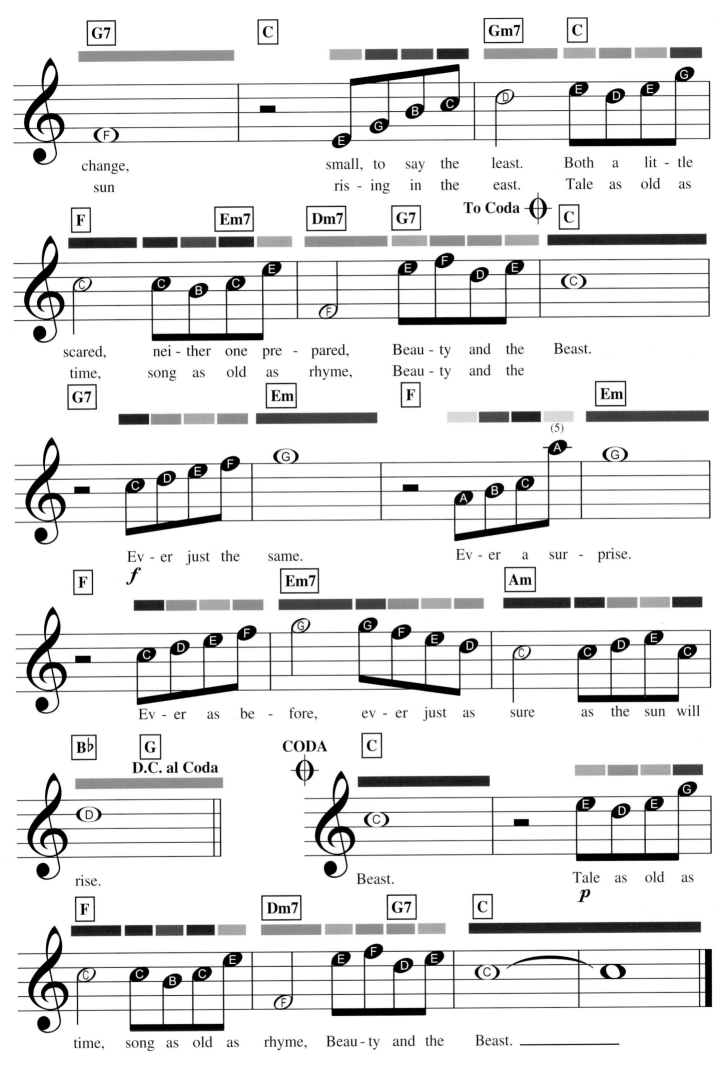

79

Word Search

Can you find all the music words on the list? Circle the words you find and then cross them off the list as you work.

```
K Q H D A C A P O Y Q D A S B T I W L V K Q H
E K V O O Z S T G B X C M W O X R G E P X X Z
Y E V P R M W P L H A C H Q J Z I I E X W O
B L J T E M P O A Z R O Y O M J B T T B B Q I
O U B B B W S I Y C P R V L G G G O H A F C X
A D T S N U Q T D N E D X E K V N I Q R R R Y
R Y E U K U B C X O G S T N R D F Z O L E M L
D N B I Z I F O C T G Y Q O E K B S O I S F M
C A O R G W P S K E I M H T X C A P S N T M M
B M T A F H L I T S O B T E E C H K B E T U S
D I Y R O B T U H U H O P X O L L Q U S H S O
I C L A E E H H S T D L X T I P T I C A H I W
Q S O R B B S U N H L E D G E R L I N E A C S
U F B S G S L M L O A B G M D K V G K E L A T
A H P A C T B E F T T R I E D G O M K F F L A
R O L L O E E X C P C E P A O F I Y V T N P F
T F M R D P A P C L E K F S U V D M U P O H F
E B B P A G M K S Q E L I U B U Q G T W T A Z
R E P E A T S I G N Z F N R L H Z A N Z E B S
N O S D A P A L H P V N E E E A L W M F H E C
O U V H X T Y F S C A L E J B F Z T Q X S T V
T H T I E K L O L U G J R M A A S B V R T E U
E T I M E S I G N A T U R E R C Y J R T L I Q
```

Arpeggio	Dynamics	Measure	Skip
Bar lines	Eighth note	Music alphabet	Space
Beam	Fine	Notes	Staff
Beat	Flag	Quarter note	Step
Chord symbol	Flat	Repeat sign	Tempo
Coda	Half note	Rest	Tie
Da capo	Keyboard	Rit	Time signature
Dotted note	Ledger line	Scale	Treble clef
Double bar	Line	Sharp	Whole note

Answers on page 96.

More About Sharps and Flats

Sharps and flats create more notes to play in our songs. Let's review these important musical symbols.

A sharp ♯ *raises* a note. On the keyboard, this is the very next note higher, usually a black key.

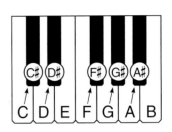

A flat ♭ *lowers* a note. On the keyboard, this is the very next note lower, usually a black key.

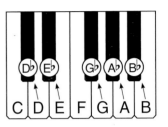

Here's a new rule. Notes that are sharp or flat **stay sharp or flat for the whole measure**.

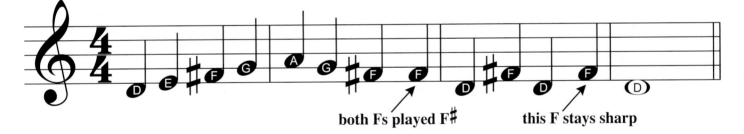

both Fs played F♯   this F stays sharp

To cancel a sharp or flat, use this new symbol called a *natural*: ♮

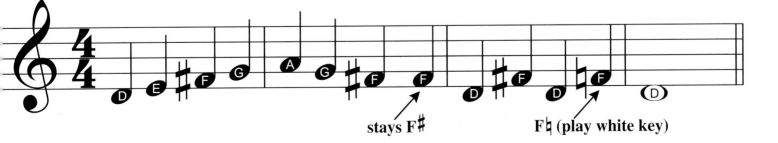

stays F♯   F♮ (play white key)

81

"Cruella De Vil" has a lot of sharps, flats, and naturals. Circle all the sharps. Remember, sharps raise the note. Next, circle all the flats. Flats lower the note. Finally, circle all the natural signs. Natural signs cancel a sharp or a flat.

Cruella De Vil
from Walt Disney's 101 DALMATIONS

Words and Music by Mel Leven

Moderately, with a swing

Cru - el - la De Vil, Cru - el - la De Vil, if
curl of her lips, the ice in her stare;

she does - n't scare you, no e - vil thing will. To
in - no - cent chil - dren had bet - ter be - ware. She's

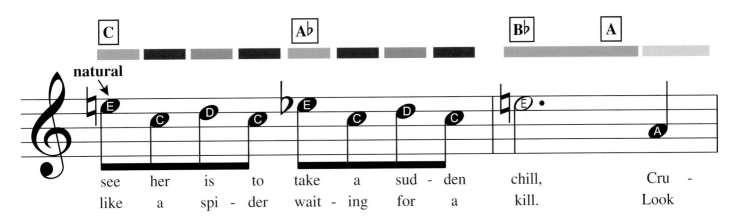

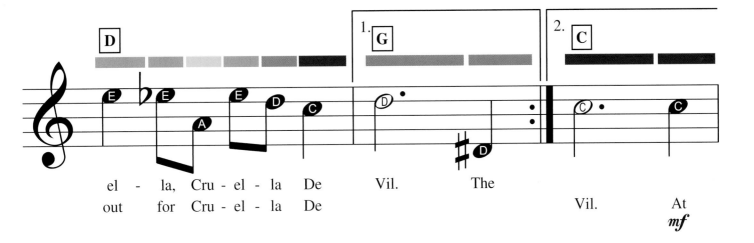

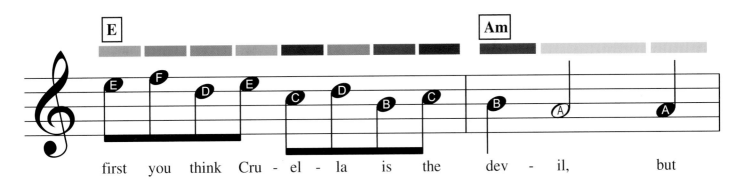

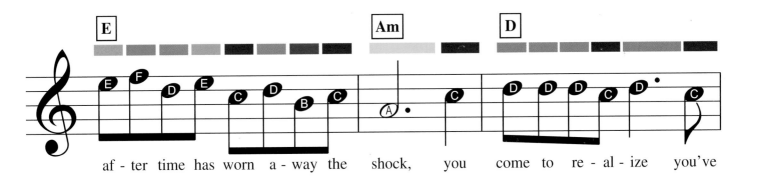

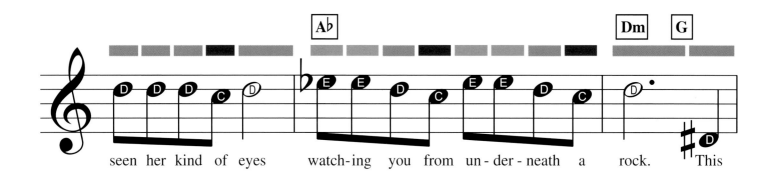

seen her kind of eyes watch-ing you from un - der - neath a rock. This

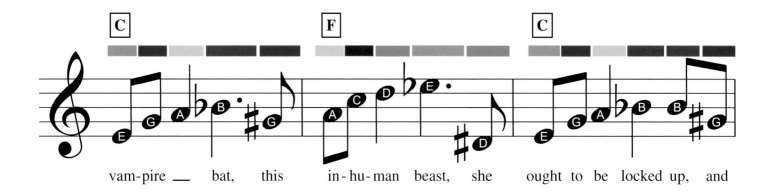

vam-pire __ bat, this in - hu - man beast, she ought to be locked up, and

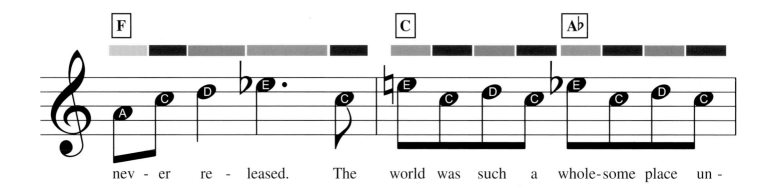

nev - er re - leased. The world was such a whole-some place un -

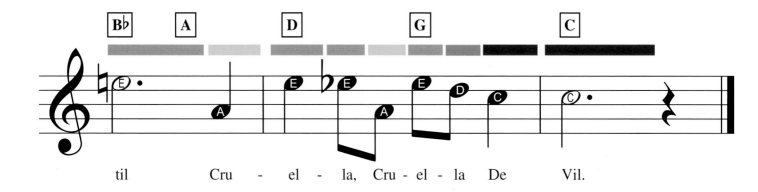

til Cru - el - la, Cru - el - la De Vil.

Syncopation

In many rhythm patterns, the strongest beat occurs on the first beat of the measure.

In $\frac{4}{4}$ time, the strong beats fall on one and three.

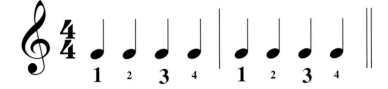

In $\frac{6}{8}$ time, the strong beats fall on one and four.

When beats other than these receive a strong accent, we hear *syncopation*. Syncopation in music is when an accent occurs on what is usually a weak beat in the measure. One of the most common syncopated rhythms is when an eighth note is played on beat one, followed by a quarter note.

Sometimes syncopation occurs when a note is tied.

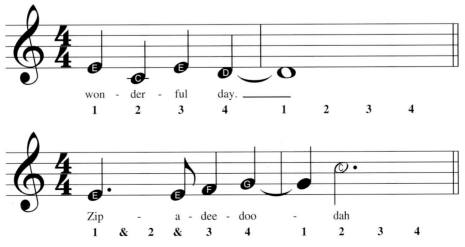

Count and clap this fun and familiar song to feel the syncopation. Can you hear the accents on "doo" and "dah" in the first two measures? Find other places in the song where syncopated rhythms occur.

Zip-A-Dee-Doo-Dah
from Walt Disney's SONG OF THE SOUTH

Words by Ray Gilbert
Music by Allie Wrubel

Zip - a - dee - doo - dah, zip - a - dee - ay!

Won - der - ful feel - ing,

won - der - ful day! _____

Which Is Syncopated?

There are five pairs of rhythms below. For each pair, choose whether "A" or "B" is syncopated, and write the letter of the syncopated rhythm on the line next to the number.

Check your answers on page 96.

1. _____ A: [rhythm notation] B: [rhythm notation]

2. _____ A: [rhythm notation] B: [rhythm notation]

3. _____ A: [rhythm notation] B: [rhythm notation]

4. _____ A: [rhythm notation] B: [rhythm notation]

5. _____ A: [rhythm notation] B: [rhythm notation]

Clap and count the first two measures to feel the syncopation before you sing and play the whole song.

You've Got a Friend in Me

from Walt Disney's TOY STORY

Music and Lyrics by Randy Newman

Easily

You've got a friend in me.

You've got a friend in me. When the road looks

rough a - head and you're miles ___ and miles from your nice warm bed,

you just re-mem-ber what your old pal said. Son, you've got a friend in

me. Yeah, you've got a friend in me. ___

"Under the Sea" uses lots of syncopation. To keep the bouncy feel of this song, count through the rests and resist the urge to skip ahead.

Under the Sea

from Walt Disney's THE LITTLE MERMAID

Music by Alan Menken
Lyrics by Howard Ashman

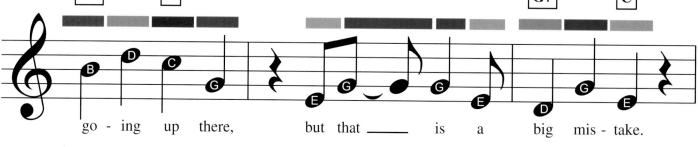

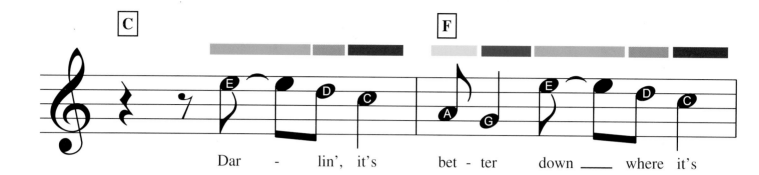

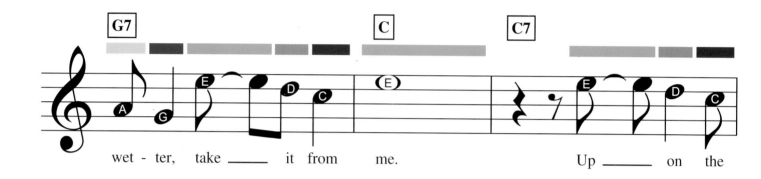

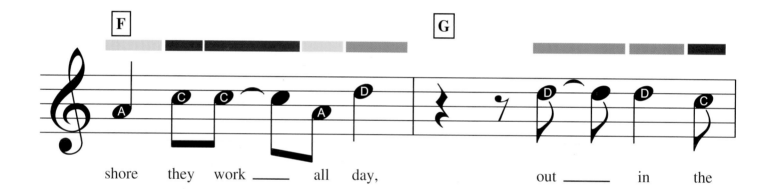

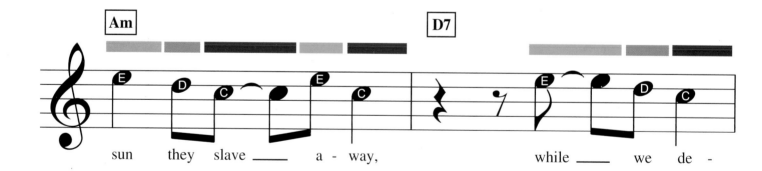

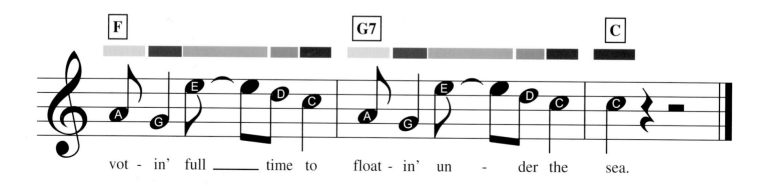

Maze Fun

Help Sebastian find Ariel under the "C."
How many different paths can you take?

Answer Key

p. 22

p. 26

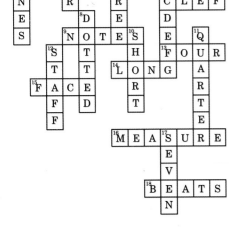

p. 31

2.) 1 + 1 + 1 = 3
3.) 2 + 2 = 4
4.) 4 + 1 + 2 = 7
5.) 4 + 2 = 6
6.) 1 + 4 = 5
7.) 4 + 1 + 1 = 6
8.) 4 + 4 = 8
9.) 1 + 1 + 1 + 1 = 4
10.) 2 + 2 + 2 + 2 = 8

p. 35

p. 48-49

p. 55

p. 62

$\frac{4}{4}$ 1.) 2; 2.) 4; 3.) 3; 4.) 5; 5.) 4; 6.) 5

$\frac{6}{8}$ 1.) 2; 2.) 3; 3.) 6; 4.) 5; 5.) 6; 6.) 4

p. 67

Sharps in the Forest

Draw a line connecting the sharped notes on the staff to the notes on the keyboards below. Check your answers on page 96.

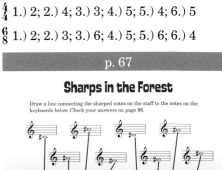
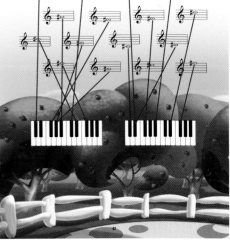

p. 71

1.) F♯; 2.) D♭; 3.) A♭; 4.) C♯; 5.) E♭; 6.) D♯;
7.) E♭; 8.) B♭; 9.) F♯; 10.) G♯

p. 80

p. 89

1.) B; 2.) B; 3.) A; 4.) A; 5.) B